GW00482025

Wedding
emotions

Wedding
emotions

Per Benjamin

Max van de Sluis

Tomas De Bruyne

life³
a bundle of creativity

stichting
kunstboek

Contents

Why are flowers such an important part of a wedding?

Tomas   Flowers speak such a beautiful language of silence and this is the strongest of languages. They give us the right emotions, the desire without demanding all attention; they are just a part of us. Personally there is, for me, a fantastic extra value: flowers are happiness, richness, being part of big Nature, positive feelings.

Per   Flowers are emotions, what better way do we have to express ourselves on such an important day in our lives. But I do want to state that they are not only there to adorn the wedding, as good as that is, but to express personality and ideas. Show friends and family who you are and what you want in life, invite them into your world.

Max   Flowers make everything more emotional, beautiful and personal, they bring warmth and joy, let the bride shine and make everyone else happy.

What is the emotional side of flowers in a wedding?

Tomas   They reconnect us with nature. They give the wedding an emotional aspect and it is up to us to decide which emotion, sign, message we want to give people.

Per   Flowers have always been an important part of our lives, for dreams and hope. They carry the message of love. Yes, I know that might sound traditional, but you can also use them in more modern, select and bold ways.

Max   Flowers are personal, with them you create the atmosphere you want, you can translate your feelings towards your guests. Flowers strengthen the emotional message.

Do we then need to use many flowers in our weddings?

Tomas   It is not always the number of flowers that is important, but rather the ways you handle or treat them in your creative design. They bring atmosphere and joy into the wedding party.

Per   I do agree with both Tomas and Max! The edge or softness of the design is essential, not the number of flowers you use.

Max   It is not only the wedding bouquet, but the overall impression that is vital. *Corsages*, hair design, car deco, dinner tables, the church interior, the surroundings, even the little pillow for the rings. Every moment of that day is important and special and therefore the flowers should be in harmony with the emotions.

What are the new trends in wedding flowers?

Tomas   Being a flower shop owner myself, I can say white has lost its number one position. Nowadays more natural flowers are used, like garden roses, wild flowers and so on. People are more likely to turn to skillfully designed bouquets, more advanced shapes and colour use, mixed or *ton sur ton*. They know better what they want, which is of course always a good thing.

Per   Trends? The only trend I would like to see is personality!

Max   Flowers are lifestyle and change over the years. The overall trend is that brides want a bouquet and flowers which fit or even accentuate their personality. Also, more brides are older these days and that makes it even more important to insert a great deal of personality in the bouquet design. Not every one goes for white!

How do you advise a bride on choosing her flowers?

Tomas Being a bit more romantic and nature orientated I like to say: 'Be yourself, go and choose from the heart.' In case I would give advice, it would depend on the dress. The dress should be a mirror of a bride's feelings, individuality, looks and the same goes for the flowers.

Per I always ask about their dreams, we have all played with those! But then I ask with a lot more seriousness: 'What do you want to express with your wedding?' I see weddings as a good opportunity to tell people who you are and what you stand for. Dare to be different, do not do like all your friends. I always try to listen and then give some suggestions somewhere in between that 'dream' and the person I see in front of me.

Max Look at the bride, get to know her, find out who she really is. Look at the dress, its figure and shape: the shape of a bouquet is strongly influenced by that. Look at location, church, restaurant, the kind of guests... Get a good overview of the whole wedding. Make sketches and explain how you see the wedding, make room for your creativity, do not go in much detail.

How to pick your own style from the large selection of available magazines and books?

Tomas If a style does not need to be explained to you, if a style feels good, when you need no convincing about it, when you can see this style and your wedding, visualise it in the future and then it will feel spontaneous.

Per Yes, we have all these magazines showing and guiding future brides in all different directions All I ask my brides to be when they come with those magazines is: 'Why make a copy wedding, don't you want your own wedding?' You should see the expression in their faces and the reaction!: 'Of course I want my *own* wedding!' 'Ok, use the magazines as inspiration, but please let me capture your dreams in colours, drafts and some emotional words!'

Max The style you choose has to reflect you, who you are in life and your love. This feeling is the most important; it has to be you, you cannot just single out one style out of a magazine.

That is interesting! Most people cherish that dream of their 'dream wedding' through those magazines. What do you recommend them?

Tomas It's simple... Just follow those dreams led by your heart. It is up to us designers to try to create 'their dream wedding' with a personal touch for every budget.

Per Max makes an important point here. It is up to the designer to translate the couple's dreams, we have the skills and creativity to do that. Please use all those magazines as inspiration, but let the professionals do the work and do not hesitate putting your faith in them.

Max Think about your feelings and dreams, use the magazines for inspiration, but most importantly: talk about it with your designer and listen very carefully to his advice. Communication is the key to creating a successful wedding.

Personality, looks, flowers... It all sounds very important to you guys! What is the connection?

Tomas There is a flower for each person. Your choice can reflect your personality; each flower can give you another emotion, feeling. Do not go for the same flower as everyone else, find your own, try to have a communication between the flowers and yourself by judging/choosing from your heart.

Per That is the core of flower design: to translate the connection between flowers and people, strengthen it and tell the world about it in a wedding. Do keep an eye open while perusing this book and read the text adjoined to each design. They will most surely give some clues about our ideas.

Max People, flowers are just the same: they have a soul and we can also create that in our designs, a reflection from our soul and tell what we want to say – pure and powerful – emotional and personal. By working with the connection between flowers and the couple we can show who they are, the strength of their love and what they want to share.

You all talk about personality, how do you feel towards the traditional 'white wedding'?

Tomas For this, we have to go back to the symbolic use of colours. Times change and that is good, it should be like that. When there are no more changes there would be no more evolution in our skills. The past brings us to the present and the present will lead us to the future.

Per What more can I say? I totally agree with the others. I would like to add one thing, though. See the challenge in that white wedding and make it modern, expressive and less fluffy meringue sweet!

Max Tradition and safety! But more and more brides want to show their individuality and choose different colours. I am happy with that, because colour is one of the most expressive aspects of a flower (together with shape and the flower itself).

How do you select your colours for the wedding design?

Tomas This depends on many factors: the customer's wish, the emotional message, the surroundings, the party, the season, the dress, the character of the people involved. Of course it is impossible to listen to all these points, just pick the most important for you.

Per Here it is important to remember one thing and I do not say that only because I am colourful designer! The first thing our eyes observe is *colour*, not shape, design or the single flowers used! Colour is our strongest way to express. First of all 'read' the colours of the bride, her hair and face and, not to forget, her temperament. From there on, I continue with dress, reception and so on, but the bride is the focus of my choices.

Max Talk and listen to the bride, let her explain her hairstyle, her dress, her groom, the party, the style of the wedding. Based on this info you create the colour combination that suits her best!

How do you pick your design and shape for the wedding?

Tomas What more can I add? My colleagues said it all ... Just look at the bride and make her even more beautiful.

Per Look at your bride and try to get a grip of her personality. I do work with some more expressive designs in this book and of course they need 'their' bride. I think my modern one (on pages 84-93) says it better then any words! They are cool and stylish! That is what I want to create as a professional: a true honest expression for the bride and groom.

Also remember that it is a piece of jewellery we are creating, not a bouquet in its habitual sense! Do not hide those beautiful brides behind the designs.

Max Consider the bride, her figure, style and personality, emphasise those and make her more elegant. They all want that! But do not say it out loud, we all know the effects of vertical and horizontal lines, thin and not so thin, work diplomatically using all your charm!

What is your opinion on the usual roses for the bride?

Tomas The rose is one of the best-known and most used flowers, it is up to us as flower designers to introduce other flowers too, share their qualities, emotions, character and meaning. Make them unique for their unique wedding. And why not use the rose together with other flowers!

Per What can I say! I have always had a 'problem' with the rose. I am saying that to provoke, yes! But think about it, are we all rose romantics? There are so many other flowers that can carry the message of love. A couple can find their very own flower.

Max For me, as for most people, a rose is romantic and it is one of the most beautiful flowers. I do understand that it is the most used flower for wedding designs. But there are so many more romantic and beautiful flowers. Flowers are a personal choice and rightly so, but we as designers should also suggest what we think are the best ones.

There is one very special flower I have: the poppy! That is my flower of love, my connection to that love. This flower makes me emotional, steals my heart. For the rest of my life the poppy will be the most special flower.

Your opinions about concept weddings ...

Tomas I agree with Max here. Everything is one, everything belongs together where the bride is central. Weddings are decorations, always designed from a conceptual way of thinking. To give your wedding a more 'total' feel, just give it a theme, a colour match, an atmosphere.

Per Yes, every wedding (small or larger) is staged today. We have a need to express ourselves and our love for one other. I see nothing wrong in that, as long as the heart is in there and it is not only a show.

Max For me no wedding should be standard, it should be personal. Of course it should have a theme, in suit with your personal expression.

What about your own wedding decorations? Any of you guys married yet?

Tomas Well, being the only married man in Life3, I suppose I should begin. I remember I married really in the beginning of my florist career. I did not have a lot of experience, my knowledge and techniques were not as good as they are today, but I was sure I could make an excellent wedding decoration from the heart. I had the feeling I could design and create something special and with love and that was the most important for me.

Per I'll pass on this one! :-)

Max Making your own wedding is always the most difficult, I think! But one thing is sure: there will be a great many flowers, because that is me. That is what I stand for and yes, I would of course do my own wedding bouquet.

Where is the place you would like to marry?

Tomas Time and place would not be the most important anymore for me, but to answer the question I would say 'in all silence' with the right and, to me, closest people around me, in the middle of nature.

Per I'd go along with what Max says! I have left my dream behind, that one of the wedding out in the archipelago in the midst of summer with wild flowers. We will see when and if that day comes.

Max I really do not know at the moment. But I do know when the moment arrives that it will reflect me and my partner's personalities.

What is your favourite flower for a wedding and why? What is the connection?

Tomas I have no favourite flowers. My emotions lead me to the flowers of the moment and this range can be wide. From the most delicate and romantic Polyantha Rose to the strong German Iris, from a design with dozens of flowers to a bouquet with a single variety. Looking back at my designs I see I do not use a lot of different flowers in one design, I go for less flower variations, to show the beauty of one kind of flower by using it alone.

Per I also don't have any favourite flowers. It is about which flowers and materials carry the couple's message in the best of ways.

Max My favourites vary with the season! I love using flowers which open up to light, have beautiful movement in their stems and say something.

What is your idea with this wedding book, how do want to inspire people with this book?

Tomas Sharing the beauty, sharing my emotional bond with flowers and nature in general. Bringing nature back to life. Sharing my creativity with you. I myself, like my colleagues, have many creative ideas, so let this book be a start and inspiration or a help for your wedding designs. I would like to say this book is *for you*.

Per Well, I have to be a bit careful here after ditching all wedding magazines. No, honestly, this book is to inspire and show the possibilities in wedding design. To show that everything is possible and tempt people to try more and braver designs. We all have the responsibility to change and take the skill further on into new directions.
We must think: flowers are emotions and vice versa!

Max To show how we see wedding decorations in the spirit of the times. We want to help and inspire you, our colleagues and people that plan to marry in the future.

Magic winter wonderland

Imagine a church and a hotel made out of tons of snow and ice, rebuilt and redesigned every winter... It is the Icehotel in the little village of Jukkasjärvi in northern Lapland, Sweden. Many of us dream of all kinds of exotic settings for our weddings and I can not find one more exotic than this!

Waking up on your wedding day, you look out over a white, pristine, silent, snow-covered landscape glistening in full sunshine. Yes, it might be minus 25° outside, but that makes the minus 5° inside seem really warm.

Creating flower designs for the wedding in the Icechurch was a true challenge.

The durability of the flowers proved to be no problem, as they froze and stayed the way they were. Design wise I chose the icicle and the warming hand muff as my inspiration.

Translating the glistening patterns and different whites of the snow has been a true joy. Flowers, snow, and ice come together as one in the cold but nevertheless very romantic setting of this winter wonderland.

And remember, true love and passion will keep you warm even during the coldest parts of life and marriage.

(Per)

Magic winter wonderland

Magic winter wonderland

Floating in love (Max)

Let the leaf simply rest in your hand. (Per)

A scenery which has existed in northern Europe for centuries and which is a symbol for a romantic time in spring, for no-nonsense purity and relaxation. The fresh green grass, the sheep, and the apple blossoms give new energy to enjoy life in your own way; no protocol, just be yourself with friends and have a good time. However, the floral arrangements we make for a wedding like this have to make these feelings grow even stronger, they have to accentuate this way of living, they have to be romantic, flowery, nonchalant and not to forget playful, young and not too strict at the same time. We do not have a traditional dinner table, but just a romantic, nonchalantly decorated table where everybody can just pick a piece of spring or summer fruit. There is an atmosphere of the perfect day with the perfect people. This kind of wedding is the dream of all young, pert, romantic girls.

(Max)

Pure romance,
under the blooming apple tree

Pure romance, under the blooming apple tree

Pure romance, under the blooming apple tree ~

Purity. The start of a new beginning. (Max)

Perpetual motion of happiness (Tomas)

Soft, pale, discrete, low-key ...
love comes in many variations. (Per)

The lines of life in perfect harmony (Tomas)

Goldish (Max)

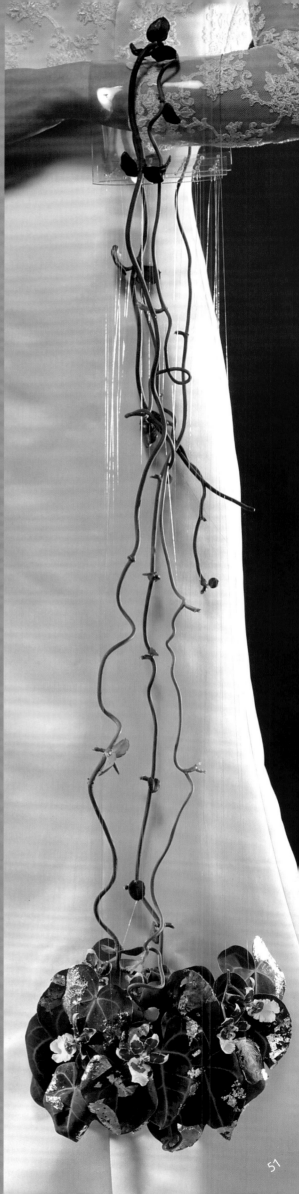

Melting in love, becoming one, together
(Max)

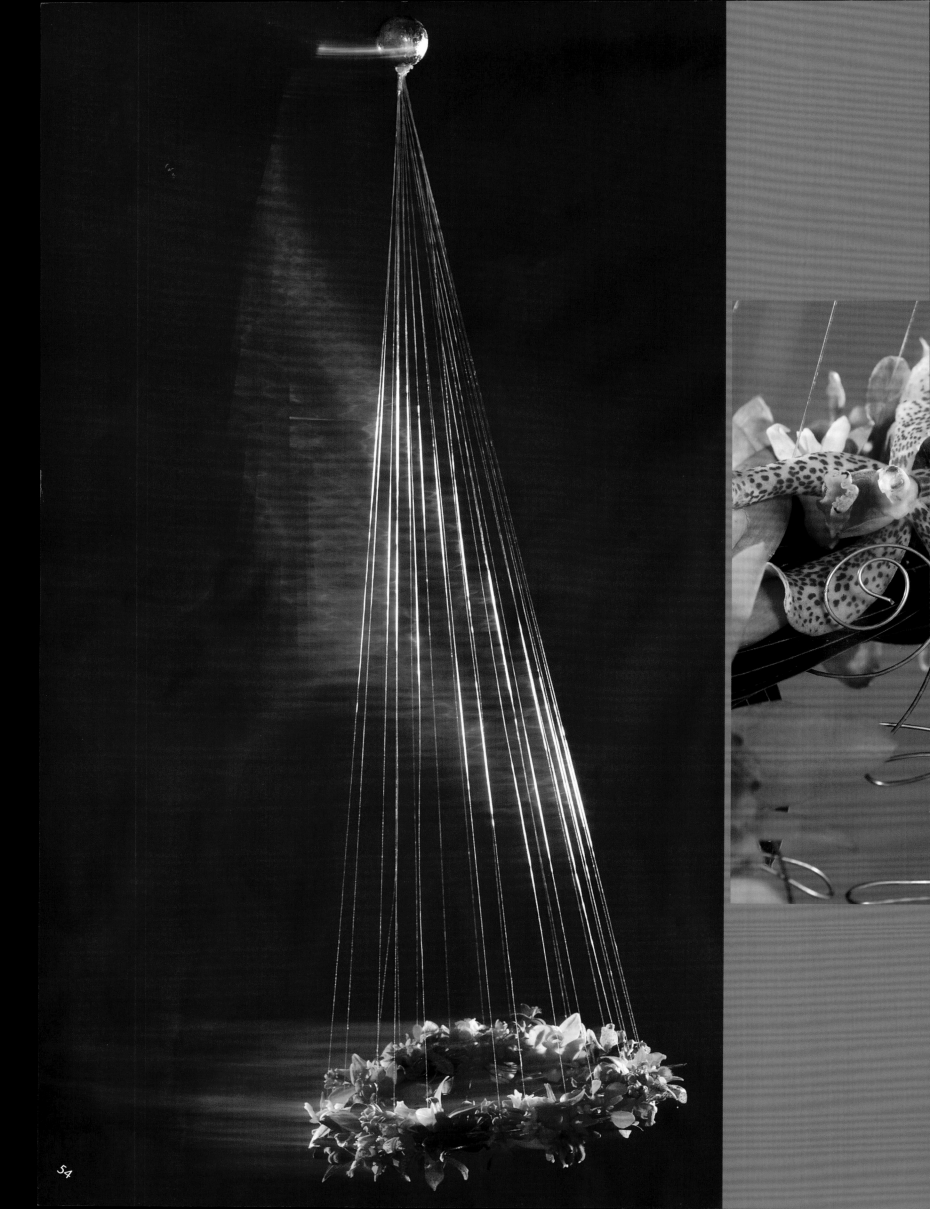

My love for you will be never-ending, you will always be a part of me (Max)

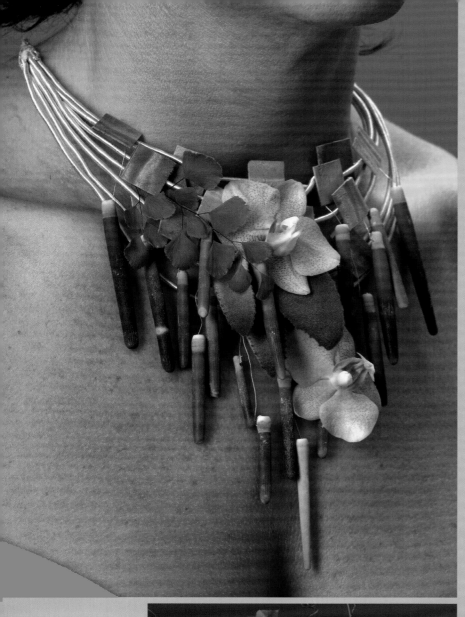

The joy of loving and being loved (Tomas)

The harmony of an Art Nouveau wedding

The irresistible beauty and amazing simplicity of nature are without a doubt best reflected in the enjoyable world of Art Nouveau. An eye for detail and a colourful finish are characteristic of this period in art history in which every element is aimed at creating a unity between nature and the artefact. Harmony is the key principle, as it is in love, which makes marriage a unique commitment. Flower and plant creations transform an Art Nouveau marriage into a floral and emotional journey back to nature's essence. Smooth, flowing lines reflect the all-encompassing love existing between the two lovers, bound in marriage.

(Tomas)

The harmony of an Art Nouveau wedding

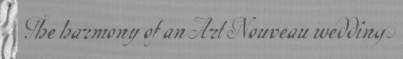

The breathless rhythm of life (Tomas)

Scents of passion!
Let it slide between your fingers
and rest in your hand. (Per)

The movement of life, fragile and strong
(Tomas)

All is possible! In love as well as in flower design. (Per)

Exotic beauty (Max)

All connected in love （Max）

Personality! Be brave and express who you really are. (Per)

Let your personality show!

What better occasion than a wedding to show friends and family who we really are! Do it your own way, try not to listen to traditions and conventions.

Not all of us are 'white wedding' people – actually, most of us are not!

Attitude and edge are not dangerous, let this show in your wedding designs and in the reception.

So, arrive with sunglasses on in a new sports car, casually walking in for your reception at the fancy restaurant of your choice. Have dinner with your best friends and family and then take off again into the future. A future only the two of you can decide upon.

Remember this: many people will walk in and out of your life, but only true friends will leave footprints in your heart!

(Per)

Let your personality show!

89

Let your personality show!

Let your personality show!

Circle of leaves, circle of life and its unknown pages (Tomas)

True love comes from the heart (Per)

Soft, pale, discrete, low-key... love comes in many variations (Per)

Let simplicity speak (Tomas)

To see beauty in everyday life and materials: that is true love. (Per)

Bonded in love (Tomas)

Surprise them all!
Walk up the aisle without a bouquet
and hear the voices of surprise and astonishment
when you are passing by ... (Per)

107

Gucci, Fendi, Prada... Per Benjamin! (Per)

Flower creations add an extra dimension to a church wedding

Confronted with the majestic bleakness of a cold church or an imposing cathedral, flower creations clearly explore extra dimensions.

The colourful and fragrant flower creations not only enhance the entire atmosphere, they also intensify the ceremony drawing upon creativity, tangible originality and pure beauty.

Strong emotions emanate from a church decorated with flower and plant creations, as if the ancient stones were infused with new life.

Architecture, design and style of the church merge with vivid nature into a unique symbiosis. The altar and the chandelier, wrapped in festive attire, and the flowery cones descending from one big circle focus on pure *wedding emotions*.

(Tomas)

*Flower creations add
an extra dimension to a church wedding*

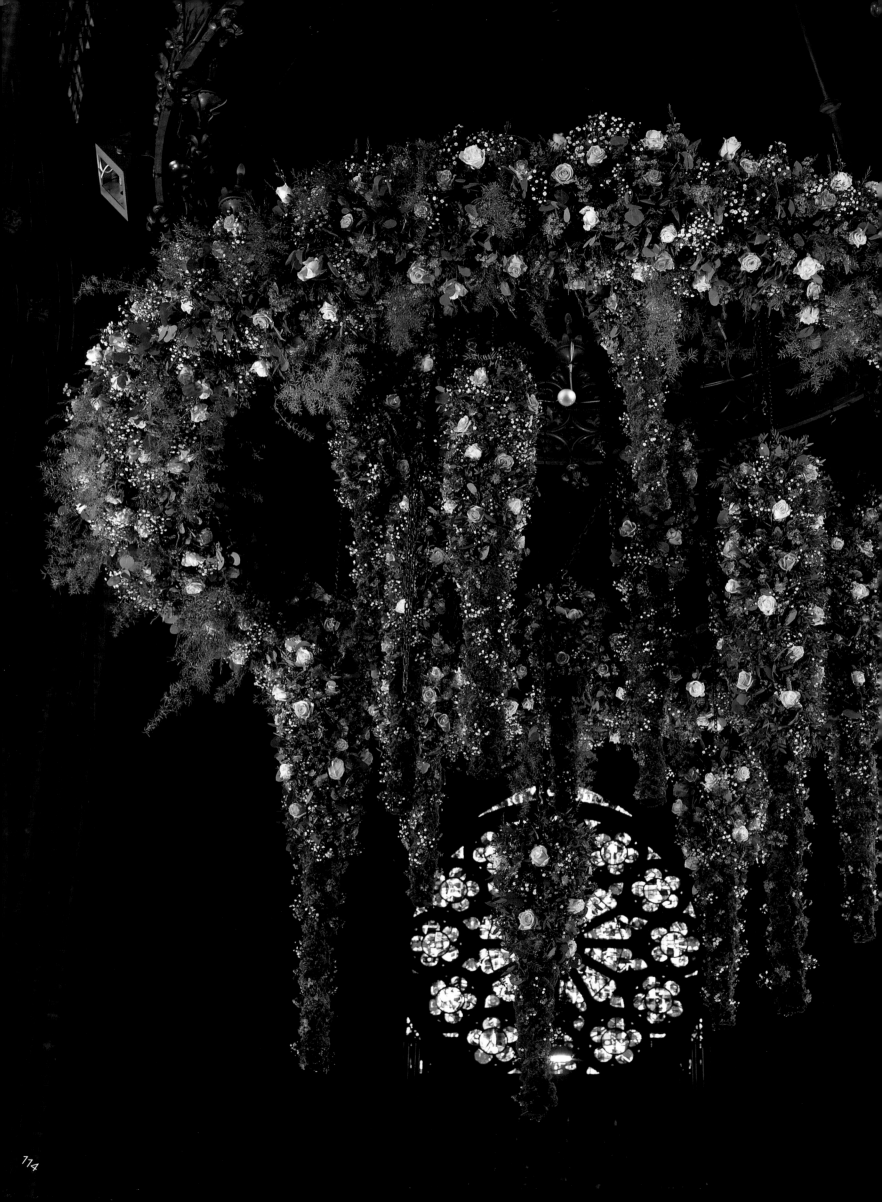

774

Flower creations add an extra dimension to a church wedding

*Flower creations add
an extra dimension to a church wedding*

*Flower creations add
an extra dimension to a church wedding*

Marriage of minds and souls (Tomas)

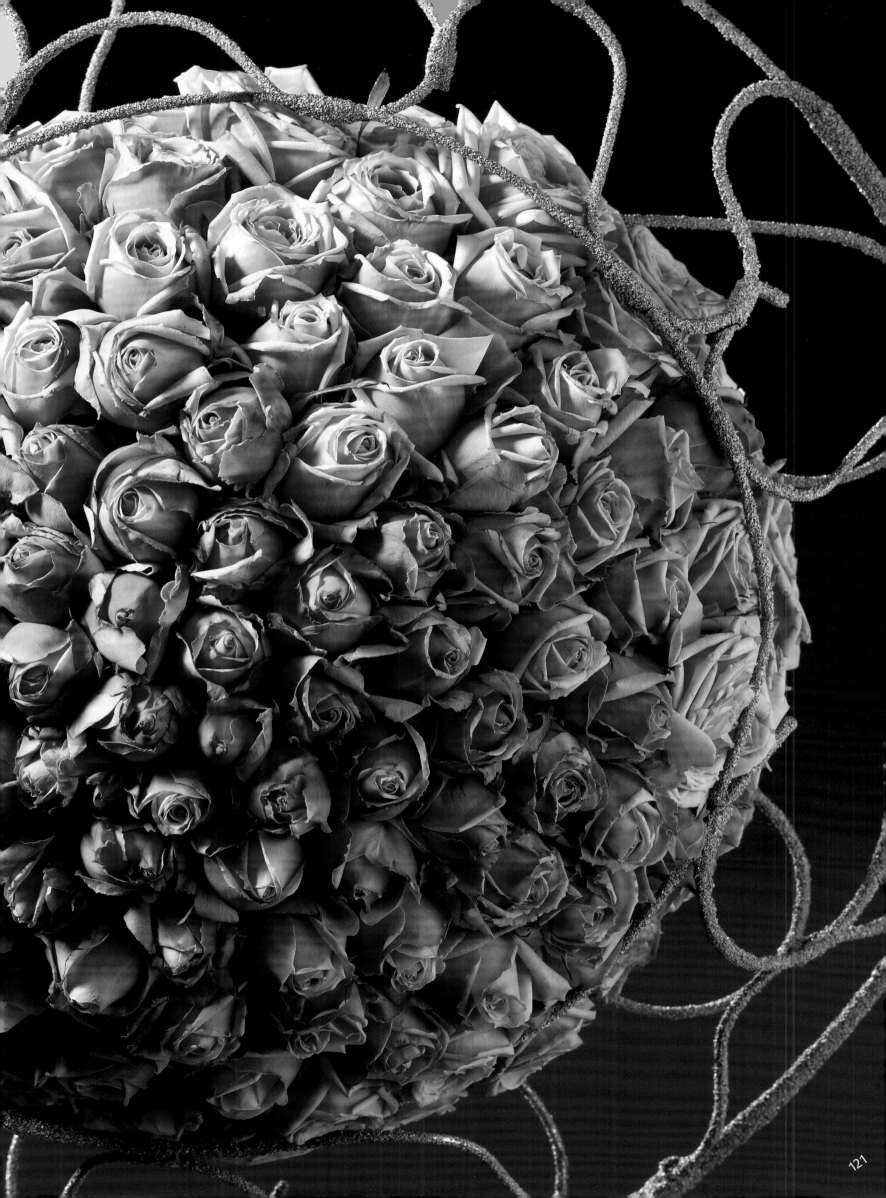

Accent, detail are simply the little things that make life special. (Max)

Scents of innocence and love (Per)

Together, attached in eternity (Max)

Pure love coming from within (Max)

True love sees through the transparency of the soul. (Tomas)

Playing with the cold, dominant architecture of the ancient castle and the chapel in a light and very individual way. Only by doing this, we can create a fusion between old and new and make a perfect setting for a happy couple. The atmosphere becomes intimate when we work with and look at the little details. Small things like a tiny pillow for the rings, hearts in the water... make the *emotion*, the happiness of the bride and the bridegroom complete.
(Max)

The special touch that flowers give to a wedding at a country seat

The special touch that flowers give
to a wedding at a country seat

The special touch that flowers give
to a wedding at a country seat

The special touch that flowers give to a wedding at a country seat

Who is Per?

Benjamins Botaniska
Dalagatan 76
S-113 24 Stockholm
Tel. +46 706 34 76 34
Fax +46 8 34 76 34
per@life3.net
info@perbenjamin.com
www.life3.net
www.perbenjamin.com

Per Benjamin

Born in Stockholm on the 18th of August 1970

1988 Started working with flowers in Stockholm
1994 Journeyman's certificate, silver medal

Participated in numerous national and international competitions.
Winner of more than ten medals.

1997 Swedish champion
1998 Stockholm Open champion
2000 Scandinavian champion
2002 Stockholm Open champion
      World Cup champion
2003 Scandinavian champion

1997 Teacher at Florist Academy in Stockholm (Sweden)
      Assistant to the Swedish participant in the World Cup in Amsterdam (The Netherlands)
1998 Started his own freelance company, *Benjamins Botaniska*
      Has been teaching ever since and has given numerous demonstrations,
      both in Sweden and internationally
1999 Represented Sweden in Europe Cup in Linz (Austria)
2000 Started working as international judge/jury member
2002 Exhibitions at Koppartälten and Arvsfurstens Palats in Stockholm (Sweden)
      Member of Life3
      Starts Floristic Dialog, highly appreciated educational entertainment in Sweden
2003 Publication in several international magazines
2004 Major wedding exhibition in Japan
      Assistant to the Swedish participant in the World Cup in Melbourne, Australia.
      Publication of his book, *Elements*.
2005 Demonstrations and teaching with Life3 in all corners of the world, Europe, Australia,
      Japan, South-America ...

Book publications

First class floral design, SODO, Tokyo, 2001.
Nordic masters of flower arrangement, Stichting Kunstboek Publishers, Oostkamp, 2001.
Emotions by Life3, Stichting Kunstboek Publishers, Oostkamp, 2003.
Elements, Monograph, Stichting Kunstboek Publishers, Oostkamp, 2004.

Max van de Sluis
Kerkstraat 22
NL-5411BA Zeeland
Tel.+31 486 45 14 76
Fax +31 486 45 25 08
max@life3.net
maxvndrsls@cs.com

Who is Max?

Max van de Sluis

Born the 14th of September 1967

Education

Rijks Middelbare Tuinbouwschool Nijmegen (The Netherlands)

Participated in numerous national and international competitions
Winner of ten medals.

1998   Dutch champion
1999   2nd place Europe Cup
2001   Winner Wim Hazelaar trophy
2002   3rd place World Cup
2004   2nd place stand Horti Fair 2004

1997   Started own flower shop in Zeeland (The Netherlands)
1998   Started to give demonstrations and teaching in many European countries,
        USA, Far East and New Zealand
        Started with product development
        Has ever since worked for companies from Europe and the US
2000   Exposition Mobach potters, Utrecht (The Netherlands)
        Show Demonstration IFLO Germany
        Teaching and professional demonstrations Taiwan
2001   Decorate New Year's concert Mariinski theatre Moscow
2002   Member of Life3
2003   Demonstrations all around the world
2004   Assistant to the German participant in the World Cup in Melbourne (Australia)

Columns

2003   *De Pook* (together with Per and Tomas)
2005   *De Telegraaf* (monthly)

Book publications

Emotions by Life3, Stichting Kunstboek Publishers, Oostkamp, 2003.

Who is Tomas?

Tomas De Bruyne
Kerkstraat 42
B-8420 Wenduine – De Haan
Tel. +32 50 41 28 09
Fax +32 50 42 42 09
tomas@life3.net
info@tomasdebruyne.com
www.life3.net
www.tomasdebruyne.com

Tomas De Bruyne

Born on the 6th of August 1970

Participated in numerous national and international competitions.

1998   2nd place Fleur Cup, Belgium
2001   Belgian Champion
2002   5th place World Cup
        'Quality and Freshness Award' for the best technical work on the world cup

1993   Starts own flower shop in De Haan – Wenduine
1997   Starts own flower school in Knokke and Antwerp (Belgium)
1999   Start of international career by teaching and giving demonstrations in Japan,
        followed by the same activities all around the world
        Co-art project with photographer Michèle Francken *Beauty of Nature* – Human body
        as part of nature with several national exhibitions
2000   Starts creating stands for international fairs
2002   Design and development of own flower shop in Wenduine
        Member of Life3
2003   Demonstrations, lessons, seminars and expositions all around the world
        Publication in several international magazines / monthly columns
2004   Assistant to the Korean participant in the World Cup in Melbourn
        Co-art project with photographer Kurt Dekeyzer *Eternal Circles in Contemplation*
        with several international exhibitions and publication of a calendar

Book publications

Own art book: *Bloeiende Verbeelding*, De Bruyne bvba, Wenduine (B), 1999.
Lifestyle book: *Stijlvol Wonen*, Lannoo/Terra – epn, Tielt (B), 2002.
Emotions by Life3, Stichting Kunstboek Publishers, Oostkamp, 2003.

Helén Pe

I have been working as a photographer for almost nine years. Today I have my studio in Stockholm, where I work for both Swedish and international magazines and advertising. I have also made several books, on such different themes as interior design, architecture, flowers, summerhouses, art and chocolate. Magazines I work with continuously are *Skona hem, Residence, Bolig magazine, Case di abitare, Living etc* and *Homes&Gardens*.

Working together with Per on this book has made me see flowers and their potential in new ways and has helped me to understand their language and emotional possibilities. Per is a true artist with nature's creations and really understands the materials. Many were the times he entered my studio in the morning with plenty of flowers and many other strange things and, like magic, piece after piece emerged from the workroom. All of them a challenge for me: the challenge to translate his flowers with my art form, photography.

Together we have a good understanding and mutual respect for one's own art form and I do believe we have succeeded in showing his flower creations and reflecting his emotions in my photographs.

fotograf.helen.pe@telia.com

Pim van der Maden

I started photographing when I was about sixteen years old and I have been working as a professional since 1988. First I taught socially disabled young men and discovered the magic of photography in relation to them.
Nowadays I mainly work with floral artists and most of my floral work is published in the Dutch floral magazine *De Pook*. I also do advertising photography and all kinds of business photography. In my spare time I enjoy making photographic art, known as Poloraid Emulsion Lift.

I have worked with Max for a couple of years now and working with him again on this new book has been very inspiring and challenging. Max has his very own way of working with natural materials and has a clear view on how he wants his pieces to be photographed. He gives me the space to give my own view on his work, which makes working with each other very inspiring.

In many ways the worlds of a floral artist and a photographer look very much alike, especially when it comes to emotions. It is, of course, the emotional impact of what Max gives to his floral arrangements that I have to register with my camera. But it is also my communication with that emotion that makes the picture complete.
Max, thank you very much for letting me experience those emotions!

www.pimper.nl

Kurt Dekeyzer

Since 1991 I have been working as a freelance photographer and all those years I have focussed on all aspects of the interesting world of flowers and plants. Many international and international books (*Meesters onverbloemd, Adenium, World flower artists, Invitations, Emotions, Flowers in Love ...*) and magazines (*Fleur Creatief, Hobbytuin, Country Garden ...*) have published my work.

In my photo and design studio PSG in Hasselt (Belgium) I work together with a young team of graphic designers on the complete realisations of books, magazines and other graphic projects. Flowers, gardens and photography are my passion and my life. Every day sets up another challenge to capture that natural beauty in an artful way. I want people to look at images that make nature tangible, details that they normally do not notice or that would go unnoticed to the untrained eye.

For this book, I worked together with Tomas. In his own way he brings an ode to nature. Bringing together well thought through choices of material and a sense of colours, textures and forms into beautiful creations: that is Tomas to the bone. He arranges nature to beautiful compositions with respect for flowers and materials. It was really challenging to me to immortalise this beauty into a book, but the compositions gave me so much inspiration that the images flew out of the camera, so to speak. Our co-operation was based on a mutual feeling as to what we both wanted to achieve, on enlightening the composition in function of a certain atmosphere in order to fully let every detail show up well. Light brings flowers to life. Enjoy them and be inspired by them. Dream away to a next party filled with flowers and emotions.

kurt.dekeyzer@psg.be

Nomenclature

Crocus iridaceae
Muscari
Galanthus nivalis
Bruniaceae laevis
Gypsophila paniculata
Limonium
Phalaenopsis

Tulipa
Fritillaria meleagris

Crocus iridaceae
Muscari
Galanthus nivalis
Bruniaceae nivalis

Kalanchoe beharensis
Kalanchoe
Nerine
Peperomia caperata
Bruniaceae laevis
Calocephalus brownii

Rosa 'Pepita'
Leaves from Stachys
Rhipsalis
Tillandsia usneoides

Fritillaria
Muscari
Hyacinthus orientalis
Viola cornuta

Lathyrus odoratus
Passiflora caerulea
Osteospermum
Rosa 'Mimi Eden'
Lewisia cotyledon
Viola cornuta
Amaranthus caudatus

Papaver nudicaule
Tulipa
Fritillaria persica
Anemone coronaria
Lathyrus odoratus
Amaranthus caudatus
Fritillaria

Osteospermum
Fritillaria persica
Fritillaria
Pulsatilla vulgaris
Anemone coronaria
Cissus roots

Begonia rex 'Comtesse de Montesque'
Kalanchoe
Phalaenopsis
Betula
Salix
Lycopodium vine
Rhipsalis
Mikado

Anthurium clarinervium
Ceropegia sandersonii
Oncidium

Cissus roots
Oncidium

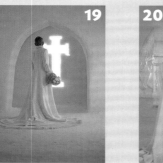

18 **19**

Gypsophila paniculata

20 **21**

Fritillaria meleagris
Cattleya
Salix viminalis

23

Muscari
Fritillaria assyriaca
Hyacinthus orientalis
Phalaenopsis
Hypericum androsaemum

30 **31**

Xanthorrhoea sp.
Muscari
Hypericum
Chrysanthemum 'Kermit'
Dendrobium

32 **33**

Eleagnus
Ceropegia sandersonii
Spathiphyllum Daniel
Epidendrum stamphordianum

34 **35**

Eustoma russelianum
Fritillaria persica
Hyacinthus orientalis
Fuchsia
Lewisia cotyledon

*Pure romance,
under the blooming apple tree*

42 **43**

Ludisia
Phalaenopsis
Dendrobium
Vanda roots

44 **45**

Musa
Octopus branches
Polyanthes tuberosa
Prunus

46 **47**

Cortaderia selloana
Ardisia crenata
Limonium
Paphiopedilum
Grevillea 'Spiderman'
Rosa 'Sahara'
Lunaria annua

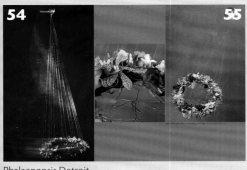

54 **55**

Phalaenopsis Detroit
Cambria
Fritillaria assyriaca
Epidendrum
Anigozanthos
Ludisia
Aranda
Hyacinthus orientalis
Echeveria

56 **57**

Zantedeschia
Vineer wood
Adiantum
Kalanchoe leave
Asclepias
Passiflora
Ceropegia

58 **59**

Vanda
Nautilus Pearl shell
Kalanchoe
Ceropegia
Hoya
Stachys byzantina leave

*The harmony of an Art Nouveau
wedding*

60 **61**

Vanda
Nautilus Pearl shell
Kalanchoe
Ceropegia
Hoya

62 **63**

Vanda
Nautilus Pearl shell
Kalanchoe
Ceropegia
Hoya

Lotus
Lathyrus odoratus
Clematis

64 **65**

Hosta leave
Hydrangea macrophylla
 'Ayesha'
Lathyrus odoratus
 'Misty Purple'
Aquilegia, Clematis
Limonium 'Saint Pierre'
Deutzia pulchra

Lunaria, Populus berries
Campanula 'Champion Lavend
Lotus
Adiantum capillus-veneris
Ceropegia
Stachys 'Silver Finch'
Oryza sativa
Panicum 'Waterfall'

72 **73**

Tulipa
Craspedia
Acacia longifolia
Hypericum
Hyacinthus orientalis
Phalaenopsis

74 **75**

Skelet leaves natural
Petals from Rosa 'Illusion'

76 **77**

Gloriosa rothschildiana
Phalaenopsis
Hypericum
Fructus Rosa
Fructus Citrus
Gomphrena globosa

Tillandsia dyeriana
Sandersonia
Viburnum opulus

84 **85**

Xerophyllum asphodeloides
Typha
Lathyrus
Aquilegia
Viburnum
Dicentra spectabilis
Panicum

Let your personality show!

86 **87**

Xerophyllum asphodeloides

88 **89**

Typha

96 **97**

Rosa 'Passion'
Paphiopedilum
Fritillaria persica
Hypericum
Leucadendron

98 **99**

Zantedeschia
Hypericum
Phalaenopsis
Gloriosa rothschildiana
Limonium 'Emille'

100 **101**

Salix
Phalaenopsis
Adiantum
Senecio

Frittilaria meleagris
Iris germanica

Iris germanica
Lathyrus odoratus

Vanda
Nautilus Pearl shell
Kalanchoe
Ceropegia
Hoya
Delphinium

Bambusa
Cissus sicyoides 'Ovata'
Smilax
Phalaenopsis

Cissus roots
Aranda pannee
Vanda
Epidendrum
Oncidium
Phalaenopsis

Cattleya
Cambria
Aranthera

Tillandsia
Phalaenopsis
Cattleya
Vanda
Epidendrum
Aranda pannee

Phalaenopsis Omega
Oncidium

Gloriosa rothschildiana
Phalaenopsis
Nerine
Cattleya

Lathyrus

Aquilegia
Dicentra spectabilis
Chrysanthemum frutescens
Astrantia major
Panicum
Rosa 'Eden Romantica'
Viburnum

Limonium 'Emille'
Fructus Fragaria

Cissus sicyoides 'Ovata'
Scabiosa
Smilax
Echeveria
Vanda – Phalaenopsis
Ranunculus
Begonia rex

Chrysanthemum indicum
Hypericum
Eucalyptus
Gloriosa rothschildiana
Ilex verticillata
Populus tremula

Ranunculus
Tillandsia xerographica

Lathyrus odoratus
Muscari
Olea europaea
Hypericum
Helleborus viridis
Paphiopedilum

Ilex verticillata
Cattleya
Xerophyllum asphodeloides

Hydrangea
Adiantum capillus-veneris

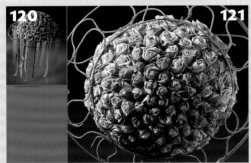

Rosa 'Eden Romantica'

Epidendrum
Jasminum polyanthum
Chrysanthemum seratinum

Lilium Longiflorum
Convallaria majalis
Panicum
Olea europaea

Ceropegia sandersonii
Stephanotis floribunda
Nerine bowdenii
Ceropegia woodii ssp woodii
Epidendrum
Cissus roots
Oncidium roots

Lilium longiflorum
Gypsophyla paniculata
'Milion Stars"
Phalaenopsis

Eleagnus
Lilium longiflorum
Viburnum opulus 'Roseum'
Gypsophyla paniculata
'Milion Stars'
Eustoma russellianum
Syringa vulgaris

Rosa 'Akito'
Dendrobium
Stephanotis floribunda
Convallaria majalis
Hyacinthus orientalis
Viburnum opulus 'Roseum'

Eleagnus
Lilium longiflorum
Dendrobium
Stephanotis floribunda
Convallaria majalis
Hyacinthus orientalis
Viburnum opulus 'Roseum'

114  **115**

Ranunculus
Hydrangea, Oryza sativa
Hoya linearis,
Rosa 'Avalanche'
Rosa 'Toscanini'
Rosa 'Royal Renate'
Rosa 'Talea'

Rosa 'Rosita Vendela'
Asparagus densiflorus
    'Sprengeri'
Hedera berry
Chamelaucium unicatum
Astrantia

116  **117**

Leucobryum glaucem
Plagiothecium

118  **119**

126  **127**

Arstelogia
Convallaria majalis
Galanthus byzantinus
Fritillaria meleagris
Chrysanthemum seratinum

128  **129**

Tulipa
Eleagnus
Hyacinthus orientalis

130 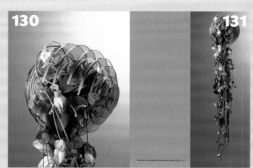 **131**

Amaranthus caudatus
Hydrangea
Ceropegia
Zantedeschia
Passiflora

138  **139**

Ceropegia sandersonii
Stephanotis floribunda
Nerine bowdenii
Ceropegia woodii ssp woodii
Epidendrum
Cissus roots
Oncidium roots
Eleagnus

Lilium longiflorum
Viburnum opulus 'Roseum'
Gypsophyla paniculata
    'Milion Stars'
Eustoma russellianum
Syringa vulgaris
Rosa 'Akito'

40 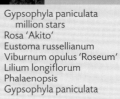 **141**

Eleagnus
Nerine bowdenii
Ceropegia sandersonii
Ceropegia woodii ssp woodii
Epidendrum
Cissus roots
Oncidium roots
Lilium longiflorum

Gypsophyla paniculata
    million stars
Rosa 'Akito'
Eustoma russellianum
Viburnum opulus 'Roseum'
Lilium longiflorum
Phalaenopsis
Gypsophyla paniculata

142  **143**

Rosa 'Avalanche'
Rosa 'Grand Prix'
Epidendrum

From Max:

Hester, Marcel, Willem and Inge: for always being there for me. Nothing is ever too much for you when I ask something.

Mom and Dad: without your support, all of this wouldn't have been possible. What you're both doing for me is incredible.

Petra, Jeroen, Bjorn, Yuko, Lotte, Ester, Will: for all your time and patience, for the work we've done together and for sharing all the good times.

Jan and Hanneke: for wanting to be my models, it really means a lot to me. Thanks!!

Hetty and Leslie: thanks for letting me borrow your little daughters, Indy and Jade, for modelling at the castle wedding

Evelien: thanks for being my model.

Die twee kappers, Peggy and Leslie: for all the time and support and for doing the hair of my models. It is always fun to work with you: we've had a lot of laughs together and you've done a marvellous job.

Pim van der Maden: for the great job we did together, and for sharing the fun, the long days and all the stress with me.

Kurt de Keyzer: for helping me on a fantastic journey in Limburg.

Bruidshuis Diana: for lending me your truly amazing dresses. Thanks! (www.bruidshuisdiana.nl)

Gompy's: for the nice dresses for my little girls.

Castle Haarzuilens: for all your time and enthusiasm and for opening all your doors for me and my flowers. It was a great experience.

Mr Le chanteur: for allowing us to use your nice apple trees for the photographs. Also thanks to you and your family, for making time for us.

Edwin: for being my friend in good and bad times and, of course, for the Jaguar.

Pim Vreeken: for all your flowers enthusiasm, and all your time and patience.

Jan van der Mey: for always trying your best to get me all the flowers I ordered.

Thanks everyone!

From Tomas:

Kristel, my wife: who always believes and supports me, who wants to translate the beautiful language of flowers together with me. Thanks for being by my side.

My close cooperators: Monique, Steve, Joyce and Hanky, who always go with me and follow my enthusiasm, they make it easier for me.

My friends: not only those flowers give me the energy, but you as well, my friends, you give me a nice feeling when we are together and I can resource myself.

My family, especially my mother: for her ever-present support and help and Hilde, thanks for translating my thoughts into beautiful words.

Thanks to the people who helped me to make this book by helping me putting the flowers in the arrangement, helping me in sometimes difficult times when everything had to be finished for the pictures, they did it with all their heart: David, Petra, Roos, Zaida, Didier, Roger, Gilbert.

Special thanks for the people who made it possible to do the decorations for the Art Nouveau in Brussels and the Church decoration in Ostend: Micheline Biot, Annemie Loncke, Cento Anni Antiquites (www.centoanni.be), the dean of the 'St-Paulus Petrus Church', Hotel Hannon, Vip Service, Scarpellini (www.scarpellini.be).

Models: of course how can I forget these people, the people that showed off my works at their best: Nele, Angelique, Kaat, Xavier, Jan.

Kurt, my friend: you're not only an artist as photographer, but you've also become a close friend who understands me and also likes professionalism. Thanks for the good moments we've shared: we laughed and had lots of fun when we worked together in our passionate way.

Agora, and especially Mr Dave De Swert: for the good collaboration, cooperation and the help.

For those who have given me the opportunity to develop and grow in every way.

From Per:

My family: for always being there for me, for all your encouragement and support. Dad: especially you, for getting me that BMW, better than the other one!

My friends: thank you for reminding me there are more things in life than flowers. Because there are, even though these flowers are quite nice!

Johan: for always being there, helping me into the late hours, what a team we are!

Helén and Zelda: my photographer and her newborn daughter. What can I say; you are not only a sharp photographer but one great woman/mother!

Hukra: once again you let me haunt you with my difficult requests! Thanks for your sponsorship, support and for sharing my view on flower design.

Icehotel: for once again opening up your cold and frosty world for me and my flowers. It was a 'warm' reunion, I am so grateful! (www.icehotel.com)

Lena: so brave... no one can imagine how frozen you are in those photos, 10 degrees below zero! You look totally fabulous in that wintry gown. It was a pleasure and an honour to marry you.

Cosmos: great help and assistance with fantastic wedding gowns.

Hagaforum, Ulf, Micke and everyone else: for allowing us to turn your restaurant into the wedding reception. (www.viljagruppen.se)

Helene and Jonas: for Helene I have only two words: dead beautiful. Jonas, finally you got into one of my books, better this way I guess. What a stunning couple you are, so cool and blasé, just the way I wanted it!

Antonio: she already looked good the day before but after coming to see you at the hair salon, she was perfect!

Nettan: what would I do without you? Always there to help and assist when my time is not enough.

BMW Borgsbil: what better car is there!

Johan: yes, another one! For being a good friend and now also model and florist assistant!

Cecilia and Ellen: for taking part in my wedding reception. What can I say... you both look good, but Ellen... she is the charmer.

Everyone else that helped along the way: for giving a hand or a comforting word on the way. You are not forgotten.

Authors:
Per Benjamin (S)
Tomas De Bruyne (B)
Max van de Sluis (NL)

Photographers:
Kurt De Keyzer (B)
Helén Pe (S)
Pim van der Maden (NL)

Final editing:
Femke Delameillieure
Mieke Dumon

Layout & Colour separations:
Graphic Group Van Damme, Oostkamp (B)

Printed by:
Graphic Group Van Damme, Oostkamp (B)

Binding:
Scheerders-Van Kerchove, Sint-Niklaas (B)

Published by:
Stichting Kunstboek
Legeweg 165
B-8020 Oostkamp
Tel.: **32 50 46 19 10
Fax: **32 50 46 19 18
E-mail: info@stichtingkunstboek.com
www.stichtingkunstboek.com

ISBN: 90-5856-175-5
D2005/6407/17
NUR: 421

All rights reserved. No part of this book may be reproduced,
stored in a retrieval system, or transmitted, in any form, by any means,
electronic, mechanical, photocopying, recording or otherwise
without the written permission from the publisher.

© Stichting Kunstboek & Life3, 2005